If You Were
a Princess

To the kind, intelligent, and brave princess in all of us—H. H.

To M, D, and V, who really know how to spread kindness,
and draw out the best in me—U. L.

ALADDIN

An imprint of Simon & Schuster Children's Publishing Division

1230 Avenue of the Americas, New York, New York 10020

First Aladdin hardcover edition October 2022

Text copyright © 2022 by Hillary Homzie

Illustrations copyright © 2022 by Udayana Lugo

All rights reserved, including the right of reproduction in whole or in part in any form.

ALADDIN and related logo are registered trademarks of Simon & Schuster, Inc.

For information about special discounts for bulk purchases, please contact Simon & Schuster Special Sales at 1-866-506-1949 or business@simonandschuster.com.

The Simon & Schuster Speakers Bureau can bring authors to your live event. For more information or to book an event contact the Simon & Schuster Speakers Bureau at 1-866-248-3049 or visit our website at www.simonspeakers.com.

Designed by Tiara Iandiorio

The illustrations for this book were rendered digitally.

The text of this book was set in Abhaya Libre.

Manufactured in China 0722 SCP

10 9 8 7 6 5 4 3 2 1

This book has been cataloged with the Library of Congress.

ISBN 978-1-5344-5617-4 (hc)

ISBN 978-1-5344-5618-1 (ebook)

If You Were a Princess

By Hillary Homzie

Illustrated by Udayana Lugo

ALADDIN New York London   Toronto Sydney New Delhi

If you were a princess,
what would you do?

You would stand up
for the rights of others—
humans and animals—

Like Princess Maja Synke of Hohenzollern, which is part of Germany, champions the rights of those who are voiceless, especially animals. She's a vegan and lives with dogs, cats, and rabbits that she personally rescued.

Princess Alia of Jordan established a wildlife sanctuary for rescued wild animals, including lions.

And Princess Stéphanie of Monaco rescued two elephants, Baby and Nepal, and keeps them on a preserve by the palace, where she cares for them and exercises them every day.

stand up for
yourself,

Bully-free zone

Catherine, Duchess of Cambridge, who
is expected to become Princess of Wales,
experienced bullying as a child. But eventually
she gained confidence as captain of her field
hockey team and by excelling academically.
Today she supports anti-bullying campaigns
and urges kids to speak up in order to get help.

At eleven years old, Meghan Markle, long before she became the Duchess of Sussex, stood up for equality. Bothered by a popular dish-soap commercial that suggested that only women clean pots, she wrote to the company, and the commercial was changed to include men, too.

and comfort
those in need.

Some princesses wear gloves during formal occasions. But not every princess.
In her work, Diana, Princess of Wales, preferred not to wear gloves
because she enjoyed holding hands with those in need.

One of her favorite quotes was from a poem,
"Ye Wearie Wayfarer":

"Two things stand like stone,
KINDNESS in another's trouble,
COURAGE in your own."

If you were a princess,
you might wear a tiara
or a fancy hat,
but not all the time.

Crowns are usually worn only by kings and queens, but a princess can wear a tiara! When Princess Catharina-Amalia of the Netherlands bikes to school, the only thing on her head might be a helmet.

After all, you might be too busy
climbing a mountain

Princess Reema of Saudi Arabia trekked Mount Everest with fellow female climbers. Each woman journeyed in honor of a breast cancer patient. The princess thinks it's important to focus on your health and well-being.

or competing in sports.

After Princess Haya of Jordan's mother died, her father presented a young horse to the princess to help her heal. This gift inspired a passion for show jumping. Princess Haya became the first Arab woman to compete in the Olympics, and then served on the International Olympic Committee, paving the way for more young girls and women from Muslim countries to compete in sports internationally.

Other princesses who have competed in the Olympics include Princess Anne of Great Britain and Princess Charlene of Monaco.

If you were a princess,
you would help
your community.

MEALS 2 GO

Princess Alice of Battenberg was multilingual and deaf. Renowned for her sensitivity to those in need, she helped orphaned and lost children find food and shelter during World War II.

And you wouldn't be scared to defend what is most important to you.

There were many princesses throughout history who led the defense of their lands.

Princess Lakshmi Bai lived in what is today northern India. She studied swordsmanship and archery, and when she became queen, she led the resistance to British rule of her country.

Princess Amina of sixteenth-century Zazzau, a place now known as Zaria in Nigeria, opened up trade routes and was known for a reign of prosperity.

Princess Pingyang, born around 600 AD of the Tang dynasty in China, commanded an enormous army in order to defend her realm.

Lady K'abel, Princess of Calakmul, became the queen, military governor, and supreme warrior of the Wak kingdom in the seventh century. She was called "Lady Snake Lord" and ruled in what is today northwestern Guatemala, and she held more power than her husband, the king.

If you were a princess,
you might rap
and share your music
with everyone!

Princess Sikhanyiso Dlamini of Eswatini (formerly known as Swaziland) raps. She began rapping as a teenager and says that the rhythm that she has in rap derives from the cultural traditions of her country. The princess has performed for many official events, and her popular music can be found on social media.

And you might have many jobs besides being a **princess.**

Princess Marie Pavlovna of Russia was a photojournalist who wrote two books, *Education of a Princess* and *A Princess in Exile.*

Princess Elizabeth Bagaaya, the princess royal of the Toro kingdom in Uganda, studied law at the University of Cambridge and became the first female lawyer in her country. She also served as minister of foreign affairs for Uganda and, later, as ambassador to the United States.

Princess Akiko of Mikasa of Japan has a PhD in Japanese art history from the University of Oxford and has worked as a professor.

Princess Nisreen el-Hashemite from the royal family of Iraq has doctorates in both science and medicine, and she has been a researcher at the University College London as well as at Harvard Medical School. At the United Nations, she helped establish the International Day of Women and Girls in Science.

You would do amazing things like . . .

Learn how to code.

Princess Lalla Salma of Morocco received a degree in computer engineering and graduated first in her class. Today she uses her love and knowledge of science to champion cancer research.

Study languages.

At the age of twelve, Princess Elisabeth of Belgium gave her first formal speech in the three official languages of Belgium: Dutch, French, and German. The princess regularly volunteers in elderly residential care centers and homeless shelters. Her language skills help her to speak with many different people.

Crown Princess Kiko of Japan is fluent in sign language and is a skilled sign-language interpreter.

Invent!

In 1908, Princess Stéphanie of Belgium invented a new kind of warming dish. She took out patents in England, France, Germany, Italy, and Belgium.

In around 530 BC, Princess Ennigaldi-Nanna of the Neo-Babylonian Empire created the world's first museum in what is now Iraq. When archaeologists dug up the museum, they found that the artifacts had been labeled!

If you were a princess, you would be remembered for marvelous deeds.

You might even have a natural wonder named after you.

In 1860, Mount Alice in British Columbia was named for Princess Alice of the United Kingdom, who helped to found a hospital and a society to educate women during the nineteenth century.

Japanese Princess Taira no Tokuko, who was born in the twelfth century, has an asteroid named after her because of her bravery and beautiful poetry, which she composed after she became a nun. It is said that she wrote:

TAIRA NO TOKUKO

Did I ever dream
that I would behold the moon
Here on the mountain
The moon that I used to view
In the sky o'er the palace

Because a princess has her feet on the ground
but her eye on the sky.

Princess Deokmen (later known as Queen Seondeok) of Silla lived in an area that today is part of South Korea. She loved astronomy, and when she became queen, she built an observatory for stargazing during her reign, which was from around 632 to 647 AD. The tower still stands, and you can visit it today! It is one of the oldest existing observatories in Asia.

If you were a princess,
you would spread kindness

EVERYWHERE,

because the most-loved
princesses make others
feel like royalty too.

How can you become a princess in your own way?

Stand up for yourself and others,
with a strong mind, body, and heart.

You don't need a crown

or a gown

or a prince

to hold your head high

and dazzle the world.

Princesses are often born into royal families and have no choice in the matter. Some women become princesses because of the person they marry.

Here are a few more facts about each of the princesses in this book.

Princess Maja Synke was born into a nonroyal family, and her parents became political prisoners when they tried to escape from East Germany. Bright and athletic, Maja skipped two grades and became a junior tennis champion. When she married the prince of Hohenzollern, she became a princess through marriage. A committed vegan, she's known for rescuing animals and is a designer of royally inspired pet products. She was born October 8, 1971, in Dresden, Germany.

Princess Alia al-Hussein is the daughter of King Hussein of Jordan and his first wife, Sharifa Dina bint Abdul-Hamid. The princess is an author and is a skilled equestrian. She is known for her advocacy of animal welfare, especially through the Princess Alia Foundation. She was born February 13, 1956, in Jordan.

Princess Stéphanie is the daughter of American film actress Grace Kelly—who became Princess Grace of Monaco—and Prince Rainier III of Monaco. Princess Stéphanie has worked as a fashion designer and a model, and has been a pop singer. She performed a number one hit in France. She was born February 1, 1965, in Monte Carlo, Monaco.

Catherine, Duchess of Cambridge, became a member of the British royal family when she married Prince William, Duke of Cambridge, who is in line to become king of the United Kingdom. She graduated from the University of St. Andrews with a degree in art history, with honors. The duchess launched Nursing Now, a campaign to honor nurses, because her grandmother and great-grandmother worked as volunteer nurses. She was born January 9, 1982, in Reading, England.

Meghan, Duchess of Sussex, became a member of the British royal family when she married Prince Harry, Duke of Sussex. She graduated from Northwestern University, where she double majored in theater and international studies. Before her marriage the duchess worked as an actress in film and television. For many years she has advocated for social justice and women's empowerment. She was born August 4, 1981, in Los Angeles, California.

Diana, Princess of Wales, was born into an aristocratic family with royal connections. As a girl Diana loved climbing trees and playing with animals. One of her first jobs was as an assistant kindergarten teacher. For her commitment to humanitarian causes, such as helping to erase the stigma of AIDS and working to ban land mines, she's known as "the People's Princess." She was born July 1, 1961, in Sandringham, England. She died August 31, 1997, in Paris, France.

Princess Catharina-Amalia, Princess of Orange, is the oldest daughter of King Willem-Alexander and the Argentine-born Queen Máxima, and will one day become the queen of the Netherlands. In school the princess has been studying Chinese, and she enjoys riding horses, judo, and ballet, as well as playing the violin. She was born December 7, 2003, in The Hague, the Netherlands.

Princess Reema is the daughter of Bandar bin Sultan, a prince, and Haifa bint Faisal. The princess is an entrepreneur and has served as the CEO of two major companies. She has worked tirelessly to make sports and sporting events more inclusive for women in Saudi Arabia. She was born in 1975 in Riyadh, Saudi Arabia.

Princess Haya bint al-Hussein is the daughter of King Hussein of Jordan and Queen Alia. The princess is a very accomplished equestrian and represented Jordan in the 2000 Olympic Games in Sydney, Australia. She was the first Arab woman to be named as the Goodwill Ambassador for the United Nations World Food Program. She has been especially dedicated to ending hunger in her native Jordan. She was born May 3, 1974, in Amman, Jordan.

Princess Anne is the only daughter of Queen Elizabeth II and Prince Philip, Duke of Edinburgh. She competed as an equestrian in the 1976 Olympics in Montreal, and became the first member of the royal family to compete in the Olympics. The princess, officially known as the Princess Royal since 1987, works with hundreds of charities and represented Great Britain on the International Olympic Committee. She was born August 15, 1950, in London, England.

Princess Charlene is the daughter of Michael Wittstock, a sales manager, and Lynette Wittstock, a swim instructor. She became a princess when she married Prince Albert of Monaco in 2011. The princess has won several gold medals for South Africa in international swim competitions and swam for the country in the 2000 Sydney Olympics. The princess has served as a global ambassador for the Special Olympics. She was born January 25, 1978, in Bulawayo, Zimbabwe.

Princess Alice was the daughter of Prince Louis of Battenberg and Princess Victoria of Hesse and by Rhine, and the great-granddaughter of Queen Victoria of England. She was the mother of Prince Philip, husband of Queen Elizabeth II. For her work hiding a Jewish family in her palace residence during World War II, Princess Alice was honored with the title "Righteous Among the Nations" by Yad Vashem, the World Holocaust Remembrance Center in Israel. She was born February 25, 1885, in Windsor, England. She died December 5, 1969, in London, England.

Princess Lakshmi Bai was raised in the court of the peshwa—who was the chief minister of the Maratha people of India. As a girl she was trained in martial arts and was skilled in horseback riding. She married the maharaja of Jhansi, Gangadhar Rao, who had a ranking equivalent to a prince. She later led the resistance against the British, who were trying to take control of the region, and she dressed up like a man in order to fight the invading forces. She was born November 19, 1835, in Kashi, India. She died June 17, 1858, in Kotah-ki-Serai, India.

Princess Amina was the daughter of Bakwa of Turunku, the ruler of Zazzau, whose gender is unknown by historians. She was trained as a warrior and eventually took over as leader of Zazzau and queen. During her thirty-four-year rule of her country, she greatly expanded the nation's territory and wealth. She built walls around her conquered territories, and those fortress walls remained for hundreds of years. She was born in approximately 1536 in Zazzau, a city-state of Hausaland (what today is Zaria, Nigeria). She died in approximately 1610 in Bida, Nigeria.

Princess Pingyang was the daughter of Li Yuan, a military commander. In 617 her father and her husband—Cai Shao, head of the palace guards—rebelled against the unpopular Chinese emperor Yangdi. The princess fed the hungry and soon had a loyal following, which became known as "the Army of the Lady." Her army grew to seventy thousand soldiers, and she was able to conquer Yangdi's army. She was born approximately in 590, possibly in the Huxian province. She died in 623 in Changan.

Lady K'abel, Princess of Calakmul, ruled the Wak kingdom (in what today is northwestern Guatemala) with her husband, K'inich Bahlam, for two decades in the seventh century. It is believed that princess was also known as Lady Water Lily Hand. A portrait of her on a stone slab, dated around 692 AD, can be found in the Cleveland Museum of Art. She ruled from 672 to 692 AD in the Mayan city El Perú-Waka', in Petén, Guatemala.

Princess Sikhanyiso Dlamini is the oldest daughter of King Mswati III and Inkhosikati LaMbikiza, both of Eswatini (formerly known as Swaziland). The princess enjoys performing hip-hop, which she says derives from her own cultural traditions, and founded the Imbali Foundation, which is dedicated to uplifting and supporting girls in her country. In 2012 the princess graduated from the University of Sydney with a master's degree in digital communication. In 2018 the princess was appointed as the country's minister of Information, Communication, and Technology. She was born September 1, 1987, in Mbabane, Swaziland.

Princess Marie Pavlovna was the daughter of Grand Duke Paul Alexandrovich and Princess Alexandra of Greece. In 1908 Marie became a princess when she married Prince Wilhelm, Duke of Södermanland. After the Russian Revolution she moved to Paris and opened up a sewing shop, working with the famed designer Coco Chanel. In 1929 she moved to the United States, where she wrote two memoirs, *Education of a Princess* and *A Princess in Exile*, which became bestsellers. She was born April 18, 1890, in Saint Petersburg, Russia. She died December 13, 1958, in Baden-Württemberg, Germany.

Princess Elizabeth Bagaaya is the daughter of King George Rukidi III and Queen Kezia Byunjeru of the kingdom of Toro in western Uganda. After the princess graduated from the University of Cambridge with a law degree, she worked as a model and acted in films. When Elizabeth became Minister of Foreign Affairs, she became the first woman to hold a high level ministerial post in Uganda. She was born in 1936 in western Uganda.

Princess Akiko of Mikasa is the elder daughter of Prince and Princess Tomohito of Mikasa. The princess graduated from Gakushuin University in Japan and then received her doctorate from the University of Oxford in 2010. She has worked as a research fellow at the institute of Japanese culture at Kyoto Sangyo University. In addition she has been a guest professor at Kokugakuin University and Kyoto City University of Arts. She was born December 20, 1981.

Princess Nisreen el-Hashemite is the granddaughter of King Faisal I of Iraq. She has four degrees in science and in medicine, including an MD and a PhD. She's a painter, human rights activist, and internationally recognized researcher. At Harvard Medical School she conducted research on cancer, and she founded the Women in Science International League. She was born July 17, 1969, in the State of Kuwait.

Princess Lalla Salma

was born to El Haj Abdelhamid Bennani, a teacher, and Naïma Bensouda. After graduation from the National School of Computer Science and Systems Analysis, Salma became a computer engineer. In October 2001 her engagement was announced, and in March 2002 she married King Mohammed VI of Morocco and became Princess Lalla Salma. In her role as a royal, she has worked hard toward the prevention of cancer and HIV/AIDS. She was born May 10, 1978, in Fez, Morocco.

Princess Elisabeth of Belgium is the oldest child of King Philippe and Queen Mathilde, and is the future monarch of Belgium. After two years of study at UWC Atlantic College in Wales, the princess obtained her International Baccalaureate diploma. She is now studying at the Royal Military Academy in Belgium. She was born October 25, 2001, in Brussels, Belgium.

Crown Princess Kiko was born into a nonroyal family and as a young child lived in Philadelphia, when her father was studying at the University of Pennsylvania. When she married Prince Aya in 1990, she became a princess and a member of the Imperial House of Japan. The princess is fluent in English and German, as well as sign language and speaks Chinese. She holds a doctorate in psychology and is an advocate for the deaf community. She was born September 11, 1966, in Japan.

Princess Stéphanie was the daughter of Queen Marie Henriette and Leopold II of Belgium, who is infamous for his ruthless colonization and exploitation of the Congo River basin in Africa, and for the most part ignored his daughters and wife. When Stéphanie was sixteen, she was persuaded to marry Rudolf, the crown prince of Austria, who she was dismayed to discover spent far too much of his time bear and boar hunting. She wrote a memoir, *I Was to Be Empress*, to speak her truth. She was born May 21, 1864, in Laeken, Belgium. She died August 23, 1945, in Pannonhalma, Hungary.

Princess Ennigaldi-Nanna

was the daughter of King Nabonidus, the last Neo-Babylonian king and the ruler of Ur, which today is Tell el-Muqayyar in Iraq. Scholars believe the princess created the first museum of antiquities. Items in her museum dated from 2100 BC to 600 BC, and the artifacts were arranged and labeled. She was born in Mesopotamia in the sixth century BC.

Ennigaldi

Princess Taira no Tokuko

was the adopted daughter of Emperor Go-Shirakawa. From the Tale of the Heike, an epic account of political struggles, the princess is said to have become a Buddhist nun in her later years, and composed poetry noting the impermanent nature of life. She was born in 1155 in Japan. She died in 1223 in Japan.

Taira no Tokuko

Princess Alice was the

third child of Victoria—the queen of the United Kingdom—and the queen's husband, Prince Albert. Known for her compassionate nature, Princess Alice nursed her father until his death from typhoid fever, and founded a union to train women to become nurses. During her marriage to Prince Louis of Hesse, the princess visited the wounded in hospitals during the Austro-Prussian War. She was born April 25, 1843, in London, England. She died December 14, 1878, in Darmstadt, Germany.

Alice

Princess Deokmen was the daughter of King

Jinpyeong and Queen Maya. Since the king had no male heirs, he picked the princess to take over as leader after he died, which marked the first time a woman had been chosen as monarch in ancient Korea. During her reign, she worked on helping the poor. Because of her love of astronomy, the princess directed the building of her observatory, which was known as Tower of the Moon and the Stars. She was born sometime between 595 and 610 in Silla. She died in 647 in Silla.

Deokmen

SELECTED WORKS CITED

Africa Heritages. "Princess Amina of Zazzau." Accessed December 8, 2020. AfricaHeritages.wordpress.com.

Al-Farhan, Mai. "Gulf Women with Altitude: Climbing Mount Everest." The Arab Gulf States Institute in Washington, April 3, 2017. AGSIW .org/gulf-women-altitude-climbing -mount-everest.

Al Ma'wa for Nature and Wildlife. "A Project of the Princess Alia Foundation and Four Paws." Accessed December 8, 2020. AlMawaJordan .org/about-us.

Asia Society: Switzerland. "In Conversation: Princess Akiko of Mikasa." Princess Akiko biography. Accessed December 8, 2020. AsiaSociety.org/switzerland/events /conversation-princess-akiko-mikasa.

BBC News. "Princess Haya Bint al-Hussein: The Dubai Royal 'Hiding in London.'" BBC.com, July 30, 2019.

Belgian Monarchy. "For Children; The King, the Queen and Their Family." Accessed December 8, 2020. Monarchie.be/en/for-children/the -king-the-queen-and-their-family.

Belgian Monarchy. "The Royal Family: Princess Elisabeth, Duchess of Brabant." Accessed December 8, 2020. Monarchie.be/en/royal-family /princess-elisabeth-duchess-of -brabant.

Berman, Judy. "Film's Warrior Queen." John Hopkins Magazine, Fall 2019. hub.jhu.edu/magazine/2019/fall /devika-bhise-lakshmibai-warrior -queen-jhansi.

Bernardi, Gabriella. "The Unforgotten Sisters: Sonduk, the Astronomer Queen." Cosmos, March 28, 2018.

CosmosMagazine.com/space/the -unforgotten-sisters-sonduk-the -astronomer-queen.

Clark, Emily. "Memories of Women." Virginia Quarterly Review: A National Journal of Literature and Discussion 7, no. 3 (Summer 1931); published online March 31, 2010. VQRonline .org/memories-women.

Countess Lonyay. Bain News Service, May 23, 1918 [from photo dated 1913]. LOC.gov/item/2014693004.

"Countess Lonyay Inventor: Patents a Combination of Chafing Dish and Lamp—To Be Put on Market." New York Times, March 17, 1908. NYTimes .com.

Dalla Bona, Camilla. "Princess Dr. Nisreen el-Hashemite 'We Are Doing It for the Girls So They Will Have a Better Future.'" Istituto Italiano di Tecnologia, February 11, 2020. OpenTalk.iit.it/founder-of-the -international-day-of-women-and -girls-in-science.

Davis, Caris. "Japan's Princess Kako Delivers Her First Speech—in Sign Language!" People, September 26, 2015. People.com/royals/japans -princess-kako-delivers-her-first -speech-in-sign-language.

Editors of Encyclopaedia Britannica. "Lakshmi Bai." Encyclopaedia Britannica, November 15, 2020. Britannica.com/biography/Lakshmi -Bai.

Friel, Mikhaila. "The Queen, Kate Middleton, and the Duchess of Cornwall Wore Tiaras to a Buckingham Palace Reception. Here's Why Only Some Members of the Royal Family Are Allowed to Wear

Them." Insider, December 12, 2019. Insider.com/why-some-royal-family -members-can-wear-crowns-and -tiaras-2019-3.

Hawkins, Kat, ed. "Queen Amina: Nigerian Warrior Queen." BBC News, July 25, 2018. Video, 1:37. BBC.com/news/av /world-africa-44888718.

Hemidach, Amjad. "Eight Key Characteristics about Princess Lalla Salma." MoroccoWorldNews.com, June 9, 2016.

HRH Princess Haya Bint al-Hussein, Official Website. "Faster, Haya, Stronger." September 1, 2010. PrincessHaya.net/english/media -center/interviews/faster-haya -stronger.

HRH Princess Haya Bint al-Hussein, Official Website. "Women and Horses." August 25, 2005. PrincessHaya.net/english/media -center/interviews/women-and -horses.

HSH Princess Charlene. "Biography." Palais Princier de Monaco. Accessed December 8, 2020. Palais.mc/en /princely-family/h-s-h-princess -charlene/biography-1-6.html.

Imperial Household Agency. "Their Imperial Highnesses Crown Prince and Crown Princess Akishino and Their Family." Accessed December 8, 2020. kunaicho.go.jp/e-about /history/history03.html.

International Day of Women and Girls in Science. "HRH Princess Dr. Nisreen el-Hashemite." Royal Academy of Science International Trust. Accessed December 8, 2020. WomeninScienceDay.org /scienceprincess.html.

Kelly, Monica. "Princess Diana in Washington DC, 1996." The Froth and Bubble Foundation for Food Assistance, January 29, 2018. FrothandBubbleFoundation.org /princess-diana/princess-diana -washington-dc-1996.

Lewis, Robert. "Anne, the Princess Royal." *Encyclopaedia Britannica*, August 11, 2020. Britannica.com/biography /Princess-Anne-British-royal.

Locker, Melissa. "'We're Behind You Every Step of the Way.' Meghan Markle Has an Inspiring Message for Young Women." *Time*, October 11, 2019. Time.com/5697379/meghan-markle -inspirational-video.

Meeks, Lori. "Survival and Salvation in the Heike monogatari: Reassessing the Legacy of Kenreimon'in." In *Lovable Losers: The Heike in Action and Memory*, edited by Mikael S. Adolphson and Anne Commons. University of Hawai'i Press, 2015. Essay synopsis at DOI.org/10.21313 /hawaii/9780824846756.003.0008.

Menzies, Grant. "Marisha: Grand Duchess Marie Pavlovna of Russia (1890–1958)." Alexander Palace Time Machine. Accessed December 8, 2020. AlexanderPalace.org/palace /mariepavlovna.html.

Mikelbank, Peter. "Prince Albert on His Surprising Neighbors—Sister Princess Stéphanie's Elephants!: 'She Takes Great Care of Them.'" *People*, July 28, 2017. People.com/royals /prince-albert-talks-about-princess -stephanie-elephants.

Mtongana, Lindy. "Swaziland's Princess Is Also a Pashu Rapper and Singer." CGTN Africa, October 2, 2015. YouTube.com/watch?v=iOATAO 78kLY.

Owen, James. "Tomb of Maya Queen Found—'Lady Snake Lord' Ruled Centipede Kingdom." *National Geographic*, October 4, 2012. NationalGeographic.com /news/2012/10/121004-tomb-maya -warrior-queen-science-archaeology.

Petit, Stephanie. "Kate Middleton and Prince William Are Back to Work after Prince Charles' Birthday Bash." *People*, November 15, 2018. People .com/royals/kate-middleton-prince -william-combat-cyberbullying.

Planetary Data System. "5242 Kenreimonin." National Aeronautics and Space Administration, July 2020. PDS.NASA.gov.

Porter, Brandon. "Kate Middleton the New Duchess of Field Hockey." Sports Unlimited, March 16, 2012. Blog. SportsUnlimitedInc.com/kate -middleton-the-new-duchess-of -field-hockey.

Princess Alia Foundation. "Al Ma'wa for Nature and Wildlife." Accessed December 8, 2020. PrincessAliaFoundation.org.

Princess Maja von Hohenzollern. "About." Accessed December 8, 2020. Prinzessin-von-Hohenzollern.de /about.

Pryke, Louise. "Hidden Women of History: Ennigaldi-Nanna, Curator of the World's First Museum." TheConversation.com, May 21, 2019.

Publishers Weekly. Review of *Elizabeth of Toro: The Odyssey of an African Princess: An Autobiography* by Elizabeth of Toro. *Publishers Weekly*, January 1, 1989. PublishersWeekly .com/978-0-671-67395-6.

Roberts, Kayleigh. "Kate Middleton Was 'Desperately Unhappy' and Tortured by Bullies at Her First Secondary School, Downe House." *Marie Claire*, March 10, 2019. MarieClaire.com /celebrity/a26771976/kate-middleton -bullied-downe-house-details.

Rockett, Andrew. "Queen Seondeok of Silla." In *Badass Female Rulers*, Traditional East Asia, LEADR, Michigan State University. Accessed December 8, 2020. projects.leadr.msu .edu/traditionaleastasia/exhibits /show/badass-female-rulers.

St. Clair, Jeff. "Exploradio: The Mayan Queen." WKSU, November 5, 2012. Archive.WKSU.org/news/feature /exploradio/33615.

Trescott, Jacqueline. "Uganda's Diplomat Royal." *Washington Post*, May 27, 1987. WashingtonPost.com.

University of Oxford Japan Office. "Princess Akiko of Mikasa has written a book about her experiences at Oxford and it was published last Friday." Facebook, January 20, 2015. Facebook.com/OxfordUniversity JapanOffice/posts/163033544719 4913.

Victoria, Helena Augusta. *Alice, Grand Duchess of Hesse, Princess of Great Britain and Ireland: Biographical Sketch and Letters*. New York: G. P. Putnam's Sons, 1885. Gutenberg.org /files/60880/60880-h/60880-h.htm.

Wagner, Laura. "Dutch Princess Bikes to First Day of Public School." NPR.org, August 24, 2015.

Whitehead, Joanna. "Prince Philip Death: Who Was Princess Alice and Did an Interview with the Media Really Change Public Perceptions of Her?" Independent.co.uk, June 10, 2020.

World Business Angels Investment Forum. "HRH Princess Dr. Nisreen El-Hashemite." Accessed December 8, 2020. WBAF2020.istanbul/Speaker /Detail/HRH-Princess-Dr-Nisreen -ElHashemite/201.

World Heritage Encyclopedia. "Taira no Tokuko." Project Gutenberg Self -Publishing Press. Accessed December 8, 2020. self.gutenberg.org/ article/whebn0014017214/taira%20 no%20tokuko.

Yad Vashem. "Princess Alice." Yad Vashem: The World Holocaust Remembrance Center. Accessed December 8, 2020. YadVashem.org/righteous/stories /princess-alice.